MW01657044

Reflections on The Passion

Poems, Reflections, and Prayers on the Suffering and Death of Jesus

www.XulonPress.com

xulon PRESS

Copyright © 2004 by www.XulonPress.com

Reflections on The Passion
by www.XulonPress.com

Printed in the United States of America

ISBN 1-594674-24-8

All rights reserved. No part of this publication may be reproduced or transmitted in any form or by any means without written permission of the publisher.

Scripture taken from The HOLY BIBLE, NEW INTERNATIONAL VERSION®. NIV®. Copyright © 1973, 1978, 1984 by International Bible Society. Used by permission of Zondervan. All rights reserved; and the King James Version.

Introduction

The reflections in this book were written by Christian authors who submitted their works to www.XulonPress.com. They were selected due to their originality, creativity, and overall quality of writing. The topic is, of course, the passion and suffering our Lord and Savior, Jesus Christ. We hope you will discover deeper meaning in the passion of Jesus through this book, that it will inspire you toward a closer walk with Him.

Saviour Supreme

Olalekan Aiyegbusi

A saviour like no other
compassionate like no brother
radiating love that reaches
no matter the depth of the ditches
to one lost, tired and weary

A saviour with a touch so tender
no mother can ever render
the effect on a man's being
of an everlasting transformation within
a regeneration of the spirit

The Peak of the Passion

Akinwale Akindiya

In all that has been said about the suffering of Jesus before and during his crucifixion, little has been said about the peak of his passion. His greatest suffering was not the beating, humiliation, or nailing. The climax of his sufferings came when he shouted' my God, my God, why has thou forsaken me'. It was at the point when darkness engulfed his soul as the Father turned his back to a Son who had become the sin of the whole world.

For Jesus who had in eternity past dwelled in the presence of the Father continuously, it was an unbearable agony to be forsaken by Him. It was probably what troubled Jesus most as He agonized in the garden of Gethsemane. He lost the divine presence in the absolute sense.

This I believe will be the greatest terror in hell-the eternal cutting away of the soul from the presence of God. A terrible heaviness of darkness will weigh on the damned soul for all eternity. The experience cannot be fully described but it can be likened to the state of a fish thrown upon the seashore. A substance crucial to his existence has been denied it.

When we go through terrible experiences, we often feel as if God has forsaken us but no man still living can actually feel the depth of anguish that came upon Jesus on that cross. God does not forsake his people in the sense of which Jesus was forsaken. The presence of GOD was completely withdrawn from him.

This terrible experience was well captured when the bible said that Jesus "tasted death for every man." He has gone to hell. No man need go to hell again. This is the good news that we share. Why should I die when he has died for me?

The Crown Of Thorns You Bore!

Cheryl Alexander

A sinner no worse can one find than I,
beyond hope and without grace;
can one be than I.

But, you loved me indeed,
for me you gave your only seed;
to bring me hope and set me free,
you bore the crown of thorns just for me.

Lost and alone I once was,
bitter and full of pain;
that is how you found me,
you loved me none the less.

But, you loved me indeed,
for me you gave your only seed;
to bring me hope and set me free,
you bore the crown of thorns just for me.

You bore the cross of death,
that I may be freed from it;
to give me life you gave yours,
you wore the crown of thorns;
and bled the blood of life,
just for me!

The Final Word

Brett Anderson

✠

"It is finished!"
Words spoken, No, shouted, from a death bed.
Following the pronouncement of having been forsaken.
Left alone, deserted, strung out to die.
Calling for a father who has turned his back
Unable to cast his eyes on a son so full of disappointments,
Shame.
Broken dreams; shattered hopes.
What had become out of all that was possible.
And so, "It is finished" - signaling the end, the final deathblow?

But wait one final move...
The twist occurs!
Hands are revealed
Pointing towards a long-held thought-out plan.
Victor is shown as victim
Vanquished emerges Victorious
In this new light "It is finished" is seen
Not as the loser's last bid cry of defeat
But as a new "In the beginning..."

Fragrant Passion

Kimberli Ayers

Matthew 26:7 KJV

> There came unto Him a woman having an alabaster box of very precious ointment, and poured it on His head, as he sat at meat.

Jesus sat in the house of Simon, aware that His time on earth was short. He had told His disciples that He would be crucified and raised from the dead, but none seemed to believe. However, this woman seemed to understand that Jesus would willingly suffer a brutal death for our redemption from sin. Wanting to minister unto Him, she poured costly ointment over His head. The fragrance of her love filled the room.

Matthew 26:8-12 KJV

> But when His disciples saw it, they had indignation saying, "To what purpose is this waste? For this ointment might have been sold for much, and given to the poor." When Jesus understood it, He said unto them, Why trouble ye the woman? For she hath wrought a good work upon me. For ye have the poor always with you; but Me ye have not always. For in that she hath poured this ointment on My body, she did it for My burial.

Readily, she sacrificed to serve Jesus in His time of need. Criticism and rebuke could not subdue her passionate worship of her Savior. His appreciation was revealed as He proclaimed these words.

Matthew 26:13 KJV

> Verily I say unto you, Whosesoever this gospel shall be preached in the whole world, there shall also this, that this woman hath done, be told for a memorial of her.

Jesus knows our every breath is a fragrant offering poured out to Him. Others may not understand the value of our adoration, but may our willingness to boldly be obedient to Jesus, allow others to accept Him as their Savior.

"The High Calling of Christ"

Victor Baxter

I was picked to be persecuted.
Called to be condemned.
Set aside to be scrutinized.
That I might identify with Him.

Toil in and toil out,
I lift my cry without a doubt.
With feet in shackles and hands in cuffs,
but El Shaddai is more than enough.

To keep me grounded on this Rock I stand,
for I know whom I believe THE GREAT I AM!
Your persecution is petty.
Your condemnation is coy.
Your scrutinizing is sanctifying
For it compares not
to my future joy.

Reflection on the Passion of Jesus

Mark Beaird

There is nothing so inexplicably offensive to the mind of human goodness and self-imposed religious zeal than the passion of Jesus Christ. Although there is much talk among humanity of evolution, moral uprightness and intellectual enlightenment, the blood of Christ, the cross, and the crown of thorns all serve to indict humanity's insufficient offerings.

In our attempts to either bypass accountability to God or to be considered "good enough" for His divine love and provision, carnal works are seen for the cheap and meaningless deeds that they are. At the sight of the cross, humanity has often sought to avert its eyes from the eternal realities of the human condition. Nevertheless, those who would rather wrap themselves up more tightly in a cloak of self-righteousness and turn away from the truth of our need of a Savior will find that the ragged and filthy garment in which they have taken refuge will ultimately leave them exposed to the cold winds of an eternal reality.

It was for each of us that Jesus died. Thus, no matter how humanity seeks to muffle the sounds of the whip or the groans of agony from the Savior's lips, it cannot shut them out.

Do what you will with Him and His sacrificial offering, the truth remains: He will not relent; reality looms too immense to be ignored. "God has made this Jesus, whom you crucified, both Lord and Christ." Acts 2:36 NIV

Through the Eyes of an Apostle

Karen Bellomo

When I looked in the eyes of the Lord, his love pierced through me like a sword. His eyes were gentle as a dove yet burning with eternal love. I saw His passion and His pain, I saw the longing in His veins, I saw him die for you and me, upon a cross at Calvary.

I've suffered

Valerie A. Blessing

I've suffered so you won't have to walk barefoot in the wilderness.
I've suffered so you won't have to beg for food in the street.

I taught you how to love your neighbors and your enemies.
I taught you how to share your wealth with the poor.

You claim you believe in the Word of my Father.
For you speak scriptures from the tips of your tongue.
You claim you believe in my return on the last day.
For you sing praises from the backs of your throat.

Yet, you live like a thief in the night.
Ready to steal, kill, and destroy my lamb and my sheep.

Why must you sell your inheritance to the darkness?
So you may buy man-made riches in the day.

I departed from you so you may receive the Holy Spirit.
For you seek guidance when your eyes are blinded by the sun.

I came knowing of my persecution.
I came knowing of my fate.
I love you more now than ever before.
I've proved it with the piercing of my flesh.

Love Letter from the Father

Jill Boyce

My Child,

I have something to tell you. I've wanted to say this for a long time. I love you.

I know it's hard to believe the God of the universe loves you—one of many billions and billions of people on the earth—but I do. I know exactly how many hairs there are on your head. I remember when you were born, when you said your first word, when you took your first step. I was taking it all in like a proud Father. I was with you in the hard times, in the growing-up times, and in the good times. I have a plan for your life, and it's to bless you. I would never want to harm you. If you get to know Me, you'll discover I'm a good Father, and I've revealed Myself to you because it's time for you to start living in the Light instead of the darkness. Will you say yes to Me? Will you take My hand in trust? Will you follow Me? The most awesome gift I have for you is eternal life through My Son, Jesus. Everybody will exist forever, and I've prepared a place in Heaven for them all— to live with Me. Some don't choose to do that. They'd rather die in their sin and spend a very uncomfortable eternity. But what I'm offering to you right now is eternal life and an opportunity to live out your destiny here on the earth. I know you're tired of the hurt, the pain, and the emptiness. You can trade that right now for healing, peace, and fulfillment. Just say yes to Me. Say you love Me and accept Me into your life. I'm right here waiting.

Love,
Your Heavenly Father

Rise Up in Him

Diane Broos

Don't ever think you aren't worth much
Don't ever think that you can't do
Don't ever think that you can't live up to what God has called you to
Don't you know when you receive Christ the "Greater One" now resides in you.

God created you in His image
You are His handiwork through and through
Recreated in Christ Jesus and born anew
Destined to do those works He planned ahead of time, just for you!

You are worth much to God just the way that you are
He created you before the very foundations of the earth to be His shining star
Christ died upon the cross that day
His blood was shed for all
Don't let His sacrifice be for naught, make sure you walk in what His blood has already bought.

Don't let your mind keep God in a box
For in the Spirit you must now walk
And obtain by praying for your life and for others
All that the blood of Jesus has wrought.

God's plan for you is bigger than that of any man
It's now up to you to find out His plan
Receive from God what he Has for you in His right hand
The time has come to rise up and take your rightful stand!

Upper Room

Michael Campbell

He saw it coming, coming towards Him with crystal clarity.
In the Upper Room, waiting, facing death.

In less than a day, He would be dead.

Shock upon shock. Trauma upon trauma. Desertion, lies, betrayal, hatred, rejection, and
pain. A universe of pain awaited Him.

He looked down at their confused, grief-stricken faces. They were His friends, His little
children. They didn't understand.

"Master, where are you going?"
"Why are you leaving us?"
"Who will betray you?"

"We don't understand."

Words.
So many words to say.
How can you pour out an ocean of love in a few precious hours?

This Cup is the Blood of my Passion. Never again will I drink it without remembering you.

This Bread, the Bread of Haste, unleavened, the Symbol of Deliverance. Never again will
it touch your lips without remembering Me.

This is My Body.
This is My Blood.

I pour out My life for you, My children.
By My stripes, you will be healed.
I will destroy Death by My death.
My blood will pay for your blood.

Soon they would know what He was saying, but not now.
The Cross would show them. The Cross would teach them wisdom.

But not now. Now there was only pain. Now there was confusion and grief.

Judas left them, and then it was night...

Look To The Cross

Alea Candela

Pain and sorrow may abound,
Look to the cross, peace you'll find.

Pangs of strife may surround,
Look to the cross, His light will shine.

When sorrows cloud your day,
He guides your way towards a better day.

On your knees you do pray,
Thankful for today.

Tears, hurt and painful times may come your way,
Envision happiness is here to stay.

His hand is in everything,
Goodness is the will of our King.

Visualize His goodness in your goals,
His promises and goodness you extol.

Success you shall find,
In His time.

Reach out and take His hand,
Each challenge you shall withstand.

Walk hand in hand with your Mighty King,
Triumphant and in full swing.

Your heart rejoices,
    In praise you raise your voice.

Today, you shall say, "God's promises are mine."
    Look to the cross, victory you shall find.

The Old Oak Tree

Kathleen Carman

Aimlessly I wandered through life
Lost and lonely, I had no friend to call my own
I searched the world far and wide for things that did not satisfy
That empty place within my heart grew wider as the days went by

The darkness came so swiftly, I had nowhere to turn
I ran, I searched, no answer would be found
Somewhere out there was a place to lay my burden down

I walked beside the river wild; the clouds began to form
I looked, I searched, a place of safety I must find
The lightening flashed, I ran and ran
I tripped and fell beneath the old oak tree

The tears ran swiftly down my face as rain began to fall
I cried, I prayed as God's face I sought
Oh. Lord, I need to lay my burden down
That empty place within my heart was filled with warmth and peace
As the rain began to ease the sun began to shine

As I knelt beside the old oak tree
I raised my arms to God in praise
Jesus had become very real to me
I lifted my tear stained face towards the sky
The old oak tree where I had fallen, was not a tree at all
It was the Cross-of Jesus
Where I laid those burdens down

No longer do I wander aimlessly through life
Searching for things that do not satisfy
I found the answer to my pain, that day so long ago
Jesus heard my cry; He filled my heart with joy and love
At the foot of the cross He set me free
Gave me a reason to live life abundantly

Undelivered Glory

Leigh Carraway

Empowering is the cross,
Resting heavy on my heart in remembrance of our savior,
Cherish the Love of the Everlasting,
Bearer of painful gratification fulfills God's will,
Death was endured to impart salvation to the world

Undelivered by your father, You accepted the cup willingly,
Filled with suffering, isolation, and death,
Betrayed by your followers, Greeted with the kiss of death,
Your life you laid down

So amazing is your love,
Oh, sweet Jesus,
Our sacred Lamb of God,
My love will never be sufficient,
Nor worthy

Honorably he wore a crown of sin,
His holy flesh thrashed,
With no care,
Our sin covered his body,
Beaten, Bruised, Battered, and Broken,
He was crucified!
All for our mercy

The hands of our healer and the feet of holy lands,
Pierced with nails,
Our faithful Burden Carrier,
Mighty Redeemer of Life,
Incomparable is your love

Who could ever love me so?
Oh, sweet Jesus,
Our sacred Lamb of God

Honorably he wore a crown of sin,
His holy flesh thrashed,
With no care,
Our sin covered his body,
Beaten, Bruised, Battered, and Broken,
He was crucified!
All for our mercy

A crown of thorns embedded his scalp,
Weighted by the heaviness of our sins,
No thoughts of regret,
Oh, faithful, Burden Carrier,
Our sacred Lamb of God

Undelivered by your father, You accepted the cup willingly,
Filled with suffering, isolation, and death,
Betrayed by your followers, Greeted with the kiss of death,
Your life you laid down

Honorably he wore a crown of sin,
His holy flesh thrashed,
With no care,
Our sin covered his body,
Beaten, Bruised, Battered, and Broken,
He was crucified!
All for our mercy

The Walk

Eric Chancey

With His face set as stone, Jesus walks toward the city that He loves. How He longed to touch the people of Jerusalem, to heal their hurts and show His love, but their hearts were hard. With purpose He walks on—toward those who have rejected Him, into a den of vipers plotting to destroy Him. Now is their time, the plans have been made. One of His very own will betray Him—handing Him over to those who want Him dead. Many laws will be broken by His accusers to expedite His execution. Little did they know that the same blood they would require is the same blood mankind desperately needs to cleanse the disease known as sin. His blood would restore a sinful man to a holy God. Jesus walked on, knowing the events ahead would lead Him to Golgotha…"The Place of the Skull." There the one spoken of by the prophets- The Rose of Sharon, The Lily of the Valley—The Messiah, would die. Despised, beaten and broken on a cross between two thieves. With each step He could feel the whips on His back, the thorns on His brow and the nails in His hands and feet. He walked on. Jesus knew the plans of the enemy, but He also knows His Fathers' plan. Yes, He would die as a sacrificial lamb for mans' sins—separated for the first time in all eternity from the love of His Father. But in three days He will rise from the grave triumphant over sin and death. He will once again take His place at the right hand of His Father as the King of Kings and Lord of Lords! Restoring forever the relationship between God and man! Jesus walks on, with His face set as stone.

Passion with a Twist

Carolyn Chapman

The gnarling olive trees in the garden articulated the agonizing soul of our Lord as He prevailed in prayer. "Let this cup pass from me." Christ's passionate prayers were victorious and glorified God. "Not my will but Your will be done." Communion with the Father was strength in the face of torturous agony, separation, and cruel crucifixion. His ardor for prayer was written with every drop of blood. Surrounded by jeering cries of rejection, His prayer concluded on the cross: "Father forgive them." What a passion for prayer! Pilate questioned Jesus, "Are you a king?" His defense was not for His kingdom, nor for Himself, but for truth.

"I am a King but I was born to bear witness to the truth." In the face of interrogation, ridicule, scorn, and death; Jesus expressed His passion for truth. Kingly passion was silenced, mocked, and crushed by the crown of thorns. The mantle upon the cross gave honor to his kingship but He died witnessing to the truth. The rocks shouted with truth as the earthquake quivered the earth. "Surely, He was the Son of God!" How amazing was His passion for truth!

Jesus prayed that his disciples would experience eternal life, victory over evil, glory, unity, and perfection. Barabbas was freed from a death sentence, and although the reality of pain was unbearable; Christ promised salvation to the thief on the cross. "This day you shall be with me in paradise." The weight of sin crippled His broken and bleeding body; yet, he cried into the darkness: "Father, forgive them." Grace sums up Christ's passion for souls. Grace never measures our goodness, but grace never ceases to be measured by the suffering and sacrifice of Christ. What passion for the souls of men!

True Faith

Tamera Lea Clark

Standing at the stove cooking an early Christmas dinner, the last thing on my mind was taking my youngest son to the Emergency Room and watching him fight for his life. It all began with him being given an innocent looking chocolate dipped pretzel. Within seconds of him having chewed and swallowed one bite, he was going into anaphylaxis.

My son has been allergic to all nuts since the age of 6 months, so these reactions were not new to us. What was new was the type of reaction he was having. First his tongue tickled. Then his throat began to swell shut. His lips were so swollen it looked like he had stuffed something in his mouth. He couldn't talk because of all the swelling. Then came the giant hives that covered his little six-year-old body.

As we arrived at the hospital, he went into another reaction. The doctors quickly administered more medication, hooked him into IV's and put him on monitors. Within 20 minutes, he was having another reaction. He did this three times.

I quietly stood back so that the medical staff could do their job. But I was doing my job as well. I prayed to the Lord with all of my will and all of my strength. For the first time since becoming a Christian, I didn't pray asking God for something. I prayed asking God to do His will and to give me the strength I needed to endure His decision. Because I had the faith in the Lord that I needed to have, I was able to be a strong mother for my son, even though I knew that I might be giving my child to the Lord. True faith is what loving the Lord is all about.

Let This Cup Pass Me By!

Angela Cliffe

One major attraction to Christianity for me, is that the God of the Christian is not just 'The Creator' He is also their Father. No other religion serves a God who is both Creator and Father to its subjects. This becomes significant because if God where only our God and not our Father, there would be no place of negotiation with Him. On the contrary He reaches out to us in love saying "come let us reason together, present your case before me." This is one privilege I discovered that many of us have not taken advantage of. Life is an adventure of faith, but we don't necessarily have to go through every storm that rages. Most times before I face a challenge, the Holy Spirit usually prompts me that a storm is on the way. That gets me praying for grace to overcome. But what do you do when you are at your breaking point? When it's been one storm after the other without a season of rest? Someone may say "Persevere beloved for there is no crown without a cross." I totally agree with that, but I have learned from Jesus' experience in the garden of Gethsemane to plead my case before the court of heaven crying out "Father, let this cup pass me by." I've learned that it is not a sign of weakness or lack of faith to cry out to God to spare you from an oncoming storm. I have learned that it is not a sin to feel and express your unwillingness to go through a storm before our Heavenly Father. I've learned from Jesus to be free to express my weakness before God without shame. But I've also learned to not just cry "let this cup pass me by!", but to add "thy will Lord and not mine..."

"I Know"

Renata Collings

There's love and light
With knowing what's right
Knowing the truth
I know, I know

In the dark or the light
We'll be together to make it through
There's no turning back, when
I know, I know

With birth we learn the lessons of life
Pain is real, it also makes you strong
I know, I know. Deep within,
I know this to be true

The truth will shine on you
There's no turning back,
Once you know,
God's watching over you.

The Final Offering

T J Collins

As God the Father began moving His Son along the ancient lane to Calvary, the day came when it was time for Jesus to be offered up for the sins of the world. Jesus knew from the beginning of His Father's plan of love that this day would come; now the struggle to conquer death, hell, and the grave had begun. Before the foundation of the world God determined Jesus to occupy a human flesh and blood vessel that would be filled with the personality of God, the Father's Holy Spirit. It was through the man part called Jesus that God experienced what it was like to live and be a mortal; the resurrected man Jesus Christ stands as a living eternal testimony to that fact (John 14:7-11). It was the Spirit that brought the God-man Jesus to the point of crucifixion, and it was through the man part called Jesus that God walked among men. It was the man part that was crucified and the God part that was rejected. You can't crucify the Holy Spirit, but He can be rejected. Even through the rejection the mortal Jesus didn't want to die. Knowing what was ahead Jesus prayed and agonized with the Father all night long, asking the Father to let this cup pass from Him if were possible (Matthew 26:36-46). Jesus prayed this way because He was still struggling with His flesh and blood nature, being born of a mortal mother. Even one fathered by the Holy Spirit of God had to wrestle with the flesh nature. It is once appointed unto men to die and the mortal Jesus would not be an exception; all creation rejoices because Christ submitted to the Father's will becoming our eternal sacrifice and savior.

Ray of Light

Gerald Cunningham

From Heaven above the light shines upon me.
It brings warmth through this sinner's cold frame.
Though I strive to be perfect, the road to the light has its obstacles.
When I falter, You forgive me. When I pray You listen.
I feel Your light grow stronger with each passing day.
All I can hope for is Your reward.
Come judgment day please remember me.
For life with you Lord is everlasting.

Brutal Day

Ramona Currie

There was no dignity in the event. Jesus was bloody and beaten. His words betrayed his suffering, as he cried out for God's mercy. Tortured by pain and locked into a wretched body position, it was hard to get enough breath. He was dehydrated from the harsh exposure and weeping wounds. His head hung low and his body was barely clothed. Jesus was dying by inches and he never looked less like a king. When his mouth became unbearably dry he begged for a drink, only to be offered vinegar. Knowing he could not go on, he called his mother to him and gave her into the care of a friend.

That day when he died in Jerusalem two thousand years ago was a real point in time marked by very real human suffering. Not just Jesus' suffering. There was his band of faithful followers who surely felt confused and abandoned by the death of their leader. Not understanding God's sacrificial plan, they must certainly have wondered about Jesus' ministry that day. Peter and the other apostles had made this man their lives. And now he was gone. What did it all mean? How could they possibly go on in His teachings? After they had given up everything to follow him, it all seemed to have ended that day on this dreadful killing ground called Golgotha.

The answer is about what happened next: an empty tomb, which could not hold a risen Savior. And the revealed understanding that Jesus truly was God's own son, come to save sinful mankind who cannot stand right with God without such a saving plan. That allowed Christians, then and now, to interpret the otherwise brutal events of day of Jesus' death not with sadness, but with gratitude to God who loves them that much.

The Chosen Lamb

Stephen Eggleton

Jesus Lord, the Chosen Lamb
Blessed son, of the Great I am
My love, my all, my Savior King
Because of You my heart will sing

You died for me, I'll live for You
I'll praise Your name, in all I do
Without the Cross, the Crucifixion
There would be, no resurrection

From Heaven, to Earth, then to the Tree
He died that day, for you and me
From death and sin, I know He'll save
Because there is, an empty grave

Reflecting on Boundless Enthusiasm

Derek E. Eurales, Jr.

Jesus, from birth to death, displayed a boundless enthusiasm for living, causing Him to act in ways that were well pleasing to God at all times. From his childhood when His family went to the Passover feast in Jerusalem, to when he was found in the Temple sitting among the teachers, listening and asking them questions, to His baptism, to the time of His ministry and even His death, Jesus' passion was evident.

His passion was even to the extent of rebuking wrongdoing, as seen in his obvious indignation with those involved in impure money activities in the temple. (Luke 19:45-47) He gave all observers a first-hand glimpse of true passion when he turned tables over and chased the moneychangers out.

This passion transferred into the hearts and life of those Jesus led, and in turn transfers to us, His people through our reading and studying His life in the Bible. In the days following Jesus' crucifixion and resurrection, as seen in the gospels, He appeared numerous times to the disciples, teaching and giving them final instructions before he ascended into heaven. The disciples received the promise of power in Acts 1:8, and we His people are promised the same enabling power (anointing) when we passionately pursue it.

How passionate are you? Is passion an identifiable characteristic you possess? None of us possess the answers to all of life's troubles, but with a willing heart we can receive an anointing from God to do what has to be done.

Read 1 Corinthians 10:31, then ask yourself this question, "How is Christ glorified in my life?" Once your self inventory is complete, utilize your skills, abilities, qualities, talents and anointing for God's glory because what you do on a daily basis matters to Him!

No Love Is Greater

Rasheea Freeman

✠

For one to love a sinner like me
Takes a heart full of compassion...
I sat and watched Him as He took the blows
bore the stripes
for crimes that I committed
Although I wouldn't admit that I did it.
Nails through His feet and wrists
while we all insist
on crucifying a man without guilt.
I see them as they tilt the wooden cross
up towards the sky.
I watched Him die.
Blood streaming down.
On my knees, I on the ground
Repented, lamented.
For you and I were set free
Through His suffering.
No love is greater than this.

RESTORED back unto Greatness

Jaron Garrett

In a reflective moment about Jesus the Christ and his death and resurrection, I would be remiss not to first say "thank you." Christ showed an ultimate love through his ultimate sacrifice in order that we as humanity might be restored back unto our rightful place with spiritual authority, priesthood, and royalty. But often we think Jesus the man and forget Christ the Lord. You see, Jesus the man was great in all ways, but it was the Christ that saved us, because it was the Christ that defeated death and conquered sin. It is the Christ that lives in me so that "no weapon formed against me shall prosper." Jesus died a man but He rose as the Christ, the Lord, and the Savior, by whom we are saved. And because of His resurrection our rightful place, in all places, has been restored. So that our dominion over the beasts of the land and the birds of the air and the fish of the sea has been restored, meaning I should fear no animal or beast (which is a relief because of my great fear of dogs as a child). That means through Christ our authority has been reinstated to rebuke, bind, and cast away all demons and devils, because of the Anointed One that now lives in us and through us. But also, because of His resurrection we have the power to speak things that are not so, in order that they might become so, all because we have been restored. So, yes Jesus was an awesome man, but it was the Christ that restored and placed humanity back to its rightful place in the divine order, its just time for us to now believe it, know it, claim it, and walk in it as we rightfully should.

Living the Passion

Vicki Garza

In Gethsemane, Jesus prepared to die just as He had lived. Bursting with emotion, He came to the Father with His final requests.

As we reflect upon Jesus' last recorded session of extended prayer, we can almost taste a desperate desire in Jesus to finish His race with excellence. His fervent prayer was to witness the passion that the Father had birthed in Him burning deeply within the heart of every believer - living and yet to be born.

Jesus was an extremely passionate man. In Matthew 14:13-34, the scriptures reveal "one day in the life" of Jesus. He grieved the death of his beloved friend and cousin, John the Baptist, by withdrawing in a boat to pray to His Father. Once comforted, He returned to shore to compassionately heal the sick. A few hours later, He was moved to minister healing to His disciples by using them, in the midst of their grief, to feed the multitudes. With a passionate and dramatic prayer to the Father, He used the little they had to bless others.

Next, Jesus went by Himself again to pray, this time in a magnificent, mountaintop experience. Just hours later, He made a powerfully dramatic entrance as He appeared to His exhausted disciples, by walking to them on the water. When Peter responded in faith, Jesus lovingly picked him up when he fell, and they walked on the water together to return to the boat.

One day in Jesus' life reveals what a truly passionate person He was. He grieved with passion, prayed with passion, healed with passion, gave with passion and demonstrated the fullness of His power with passion.

As we enter the Easter season, let us strive to emulate the extreme passion Jesus lovingly displayed in His life, death and resurrection.

The Passion of an Uncommon Man

Evelyn Gibson

The Passion of an Uncommon Man (Luke 13:13)

I am a woman, suffering silently in pain;
Oblivious to the world and common man.
Seeing little sunshine, feeling drops of rain.
My eyes fastened to the ground, as I travel this land.

My life has chosen a direction entirely on its own;
Oblivious to the world and common man.
I've grown to be thankful, no matter that I'm alone.
You see, life has dealt to many a cruel hand.

No need to complain, or shed useless tears,
Oblivious to the world and common man.
My stature bent over for some eighteen years.
It's become my norm, you understand.

I've accepted the challenge, becoming quite content.
Oblivious to the world and common man.
What difference does it matter that I am bent?
I've decided I must survive any way I can.

It was my time to enter the temple as usual to pray.
Oblivious to the world and common man.
This was my routine, just another ordinary day.
I wanted to give alms, offer worship as planned.

Someone noticed my presence and beckoned aloud.
No longer oblivious to the world and common man.
I had grown not to expect anything from such a crowd,
But Someone was present with a different plan.

He spoke directly to my pain, He said I was now loosed!
Immediately my infirmity surrendered its hold.
My back was straightened, I became free from abuse.
It's been eighteen years since my eyes could behold.

I am now healed and set free to walk uprightly before Him.
Telling others of His goodness, His willing plan
That all be redeemed and passion poured abundantly on them.
Receiving healing and love, because of an uncommon Man.

© 2004 Evelyn Grant Gibson

Nevertheless

Gayle Gilmore

If you ask the average Christian what they would consider to be the highlight of Jesus' life, the answers would vary. Some would pay the virgin birth high homage. Others would relate his major missions and episodes of preaching, teaching and healing on their top ten list. A vast number would certainly marvel at the perseverance and love of One who would endure a humiliating crucifixion, a cold damp burial and the glorious victory of resurrection to redeem lost humanity.

But I get goose bumps when I think about one lone moment when my destiny hinged on one word, NEVERTHELESS. When Jesus was in the Garden of Gethsemane, abandoned by sleep-deprived disciples and kneeling on a hard hassock of a rock, the one that was fully God and fully man agonized about His upcoming appointment.

"If there is any way that I can avoid this punishment; a punishment that I don't even deserve. A punishment that I left a kingdom for. A punishment and condemnation for people that reject me; a people that don't even love. Father, I know I said that I was the way, the truth, and the life but if there is any other 'way', PLEASE SHOW ME!"

"But, NEVERTHELESS, in spite of all I've just thought and said, I will be obedient to how, why and the way you want it to happen—the WAY that you had planned from the foundation of the world." (My translation of Mark 14:36)

When we think about how sovereign God is, we can't help from being ecstatically grateful that this word was created to seal our assurance of eternity.

I Wonder

Heather Glenn

✠

I wonder Lord so long ago
When that bright star appeared,
Did it sparkle bright with heavenly light,
Did it draw the shepherds near?
        I wonder

When they found the babe in swaddling clothes,
Did he have a special glow,
Was his face alight with glory bright,
Did the sheep and cattle low?

When the angel appeared to Mary, Lord,
Did you have thoughts of another,
How did you make your choice of her,
To be the Messiah's mother?
        I wonder

And Lord, what did Joseph think,
When told of Mary's plight,
Before God revealed to him
That everything was all right?

When they returned to Nazareth town,
On that long and dusty road,
Did the baby cry when he grew tired,
Did the donkey tire of the load?
        I wonder

As a child, dear Lord, did Jesus cry,
When he skinned his knee at play,
Did his mother hold him in her arms,
And kiss his hurt away.

And Lord, the wonder of them all,
When on the cross you died,
How could Mary bear her hurt inside,
To see you crucified?
I wonder

How could she ever understand,
That it was planned and just,
For God to make a way to Heaven,
She had to give her son to die for us?

Now Lord, of all these wonders,
Many more left untold,
If need be, in all your wisdom,
To me you will unfold.

So I'll not fret or worry more,
Content with thee I'll be,
If ever you want to tell me though,
My ear I'll lend to thee.

Life Changing Love

Hugh Gorman

Palm Sunday, 1954. That's the day when I discovered that love was real. Before that day, I was convinced that there was no such thing as real love. It was just one of those four-letter words that was bandied around from person to person, but didn't mean anything. I didn't see it. Not in my own dysfunctional home where there was continual conflict. Not in the street where I lived in Belfast, Ireland, where the sectarian strife and graffiti spoke of anything but love. In that street, parents were telling their children not to go near Hugh Gorman or they would finish up in prison. My mates were glad to be in my company to help me spend the proceeds of my criminal activities—but they didn't love me.

Palm Sunday—I didn't know what that was. It just happened to be the day that a concerned Christian invited me to a special church service. That day, through the preaching of a tall, rugged, Welsh evangelist, I learned that there was one man, a man called Jesus, and he loved me enough that He was prepared to die for me. He was grieved with the life that I was living, and hurt by the sins I had committed, but He still loved me, unconditionally. Because of His love for me, He did go to the cross and die for my sins. I was told that if I were the only person in all the world, He would still have gone to that cross and died for me.

The evangelist told me that if I responded to that love it would change my life. That's what I wanted. No one in all the world wanted their life to be changed more than I. I hated the person I was...hated how I had treated my loved ones . . . hated the things I was doing and the life I was living and I wanted to be changed. That night, I turned my back on my old life, turned to Christ and asked him to forgive me and change my life the way the preacher told me it could be changed. In a moment of time, "old things passed away and all things became new" as I experienced His life-changing love.

"In the Cross of Christ, I glory!" Life-changing love—it works!

The Passion of Christ

Stephen Goswami

The fittest survive by correcting self for better cooperation within and outside. Every correction is painful. The quality of correction determines the quality of survival. Dinosaurs' progeny evolved into peaceful doves and deadly serpents. Sheep cooperated with creation while lion destroyed. So, devil is compared to serpent and lion.

Heaven, the fittest, is the association of the best. It continuously corrects itself in supreme love. Hell, the association of the proud is unrepentant. So, it fails to correct itself and becomes enemy to itself and others. Devil, the sweeper, sweeping the unrepentant love loose souls from heaven and creation, perishes with them.

Love creates, joins and keeps together, parts of body, mind, soul, society, and organizations. Hate, greed, pride may bring together momentarily before bursting. Love means responsibility. Greatest love is the greatest responsibility, encompassing all. Pride the antithesis of love, shuns responsibility, accusing others for their woes. So, Devil is called the accuser. So, heaven is accepting the responsibility for the fall of creation. It is correcting by atoning Christ, the union of repentant souls, obedient to supreme love. His cross of obedience is eternal. A Christ without cross is an imposter.

Fittest are the most responsible. Responsibility begets fruit spiritually by exemplified teaching. Those bearing abiding fruits survive. A mother's pain far surpasses her naked travail to bring up a good child. So, also Christ's pain far surpasses the naked passion of the cross to bring up heaven-worthy souls. But the evil fruit bears, lumpen, exploiters, evil leaders generate hell worthy likes in painless evil exultation. These fruits rot, destroy and disintegrate. Crucified Christ is continuously creating new heaven for replacing proud, glory and worship seeking degenerate heaven. A parent doesn't seek worship from children. So, also heavenly Father doesn't, but beckon us to be like him through the passion of Christ.

Jesus' Suffering for Me

Nancy Hamilton

His steps faltered as He carried the Cross through the streets,
Reaching Calvary they began to hammer nails through His feet.
Onlookers cheered as the soldiers drove the nails into either hand.
What pain, what agony for Jesus, the hated Son of Man!

His brow was crusted from the blood as it oozed,
And swirling about him were loud curses and boos!
His torso was raw from the lashing they gave,
Soon His lifeless body would be placed into a grave!
His feet were flattened against the rugged cross,
People were shouting, "He'll certainly be no loss!"

Soon the heavens began to change, becoming dark and dreary.
The earth began to tremble, then shake with violent fury.
With excruciating pain racking His precious broken body,
The price for damning sin was about to be paid for everybody.

I should have been the wearer of the thorny crown,
I should have been the one hung on the Cross stationed in the ground.
I should have been hated, beaten and bled;
But for me, Jesus took all the suffering instead!

I should have been buried in the cold, damp earth,
Only decay and worms are my body's worth.
Yet God sent His Son to suffer and die,
So vile sinners can be redeemed, sinners such as I!

Yet, had it been I who was laid in the tomb,
The earth would have become my eternal womb.
Death would have been victorious, and Hell would have won,
But victory over death was provided by God's Precious Son!

He gloriously arose and is at the Throne to the right,
And someday I'll be in Heaven residing in His Light!
Because of His death and resurrection, I shall be eternally free!
A sinner, saved by grace, freed for all eternity!

Hanging in the Balance

L. David Harris

"Behold, the hour cometh, yea, is now come, that ye shall be scattered, every man to his own, and shall leave me alone: and yet I am not alone, because the Father is with me." John 16:32.

The final and most difficult steps on Jesus' road to Calvary were before Him. As He prepared Himself, He contemplated the fact that His own disciples would leave Him alone while the entire world's destiny was hanging in the balance.

Jesus and His disciples went to the garden called Gethsemane and of those disciples Jesus beckoned Peter, James, and John to come close to the place where He would retire for prayer and asked them to pray also. The weight of Jesus' mission began to impress upon His soul as He was becoming sin for us. The burden of our guilt enfolded Him in bitter agony and the darkness of discouragement. Could anyone relieve the Lord in His time of agony?

He came to His disciples as a man needing the support of His fellows in His hour of greatest need. Rather than finding a faithful few, He found them sleeping. While the destiny of the entire world was hanging in the balance, His friends soundly slept.

Jesus, with the determination of love and the quiet zeal of salvation, resolved for all time to do the will of His father and be sacrificed for us at last.

Never has such love been demonstrated as when the Redeemer became my substitute while the world slept and our destiny was hanging in the balance. "Greater love hath no man than this, that a man lay down his life for his friends." John 15:13.

Virgin Birth

Najiyyah Harris

Conceived of the purest intent imaginable, untainted by carnal contaminates, and adulterated visions, it grows inside of me.

As I lay basking in the tranquil of the night's calm voice, I begin to feel the unprecedented movement of new life igniting inside my soul.

After hours of what feels most like drowning in the vicious, uncertain trenches of my quasi-sorrows and seeking to find the ever-absent comfort of what I am certain only lies within your arms, I am safely pushed to shore. For I feel the warmth of God's marvelous sunshine kiss the soft features of my face and I just smile. Smile with gratitude, for yet I have one more chance to get this right.

Slowly I rise only to discover that as advanced as my condition may seem most days, morning sickness clearly dictates that this growth still resides in the first trimester.

I fall to my knees crying "Father, help me!" as I cannot fathom the thought of going full term at this point, for the unease is far too great! Then to my comfort comes the rescue of the Master's arms, cradling me into reassurance yet again.

In a fraction of a moment's time, it starts to hit me like a ton of bricks I carry inside of my heart, womb, and soul a joy so precious, so perfect, so pure, and so complete that only God Himself could plant such a seed! And while it grows daily, I am haunted and forced by past poor, hasty decisions to harbor all of this beauty bottled up inside of me like a dirty secret for fear of shame, hurt, disappointment, and judgment for everyone else. but what about me?

"What shall I do Lord?" is the question at hand, for every good and perfect thing comes from you, this I know to be true!

The seconds, minutes, hours, weeks, and months continue to pass and with each stroke of the clock, comes growth.

How long can I in good conscience, continue to cast a deliberate shadow upon the luminous glow of my face, the striking difference in my corporal form, restructure of my demeanor, my ever-increasing appetite. for you?

Somewhere in the not so distant future the confession of my secret will be summoned forth by father time, for whether or not I welcome that day with open arms or greet it with dismay, it cometh still it cometh!

For every seed planted and conceived by divine intervention, nurtured and developed by the spirit and not flesh.

SHALL BE BORN FOR ALL THE WORLD TO SEE!

Good Ground

Joy Igonikon

A three-year-old girl named Jani wanted a garden of flowers. She asked her parents if she could grow them and the happy parents had two servants find a portion near the house and prepare it for growing. The soil of the ground they prepared was perfectly soft, moist, and supple. Jani went with the servants into town to buy seeds. They came back and hearing her friends play across the street, Jani decided to plant the seeds tomorrow, so she left the bags on the soil.

Tomorrow became several weeks. Jani played with friends so much that she hadn't even walked by the soil for her garden. And because she didn't care for the soil, it dried out and turned sickly pale from its prior dark, sparkling blackness that exuded strength and readiness to the eye. Jani's soil became hard and rigid.

One day Jani's friend Afya came to visit with a handful of flowers for Jani's mother. When Jani saw them, she remembered her own garden that she neglected and began to cry. Afya took Jani's hand and told her not to cry. They went over to her portion of soil with water and poured it out on top of the ground. After a while it seeped into the ground, but the soil did not come back to life as they had hoped. A female servant passed by and told them that Jani's soil wasn't ready to accept seeds yet. If they tried to put seeds in now, some would spring up plants with no root and never blossom. So the girls had to wait by remembering to turn and water the ground on a regular basis. (Inspired by Mark 4:13-20)

Crippled From The Womb

Gay Jackson

When the Lord begin to reveal His divine mind concerning the crippling state of humanity, my heart was paralyzed at the true condition of humanity. But yet what was the final blow was that the state of the church was born out of the same twisted bands as the world. The pain that was gained out of the wisdom of God was almost unbearable. The ignorance of this society increase the mercy of God toward men in my heart. When the Lord came into the world as stated in St. John 1:11 his sole purpose was to undo the fall of Adam. His mission on earth was to redeem the spirit of mankind back into the plan of his Creator, and by doing so man would be spiritually redeemed to God's original purpose for his life. Jesus reflected the very image of the Father in the earth, declaring that the Kingdom Of God had come, and that kingdom abided in everyman. The reflection of Christ is abiding in every man that is able to believe that not only did Jesus die, but through his death we that receive him would live again. The reflection of Christ that was born out of his passion to do the will of his Father was that of pain and suffering. But love was the foundation of the builder, bringing man through great pain to passion reflected in his mission on earth. It's like he never really had a chance, almost crippled from the womb, but yet in the direct order of God. I'm sorry I am out of time.

No One Can Compare

Rev. Owen D. Johnson

Reflections on the Passion

When I reflect on all that He's done
No one can compare to God's only Son

The natural mind cannot conceive
Why would anyone die on a cross?
The scriptures must be fulfilled
He came to save the lost

We're undeserving of His unmerited grace
But it's not about us,
His mission was to save the race

In all of His agony
Pain and sweat
He never mumbled once
It wasn't finished yet

He could've gave up
and sent a legion of heavenly host
But instead he hung high
And gave up the ghost.

He said, "Father"
Into your hands
I commit my spirit
These are the reflections of Jesus
Believers in Christ should never forget it.

Psalm of Christ

Terdell Johnson

From heaven the Father watched.
The Son betrayed upon his face.
Lead away before men of rank.
Accused, yet remained in peace.

The governor comes: he cannot convict.
But the men of rank push on to get their verdict.
Soldiers come to bring blows and spit.
Laugh and tease as they crown the Son with shame.

Purple and running red he wore before the masses.
Governor, what shall you do?
"Innocent I say, I find no charge!"
But the masses scream for death on this day.

Stripe for stripe upon his back.
Nail in left; nail in right.
The wood is stained with crimson hue.
The cross is raised; two others by his side.

His life for mine; his life for yours.
Innocence dies and victory is born.
In the tomb he was laid and sealed away.
Over?....No more? The prophesy says three days.

Run to the tomb! See no one is there!
A ghost? No! A trick? This cannot be!
He lives! Let all rejoice from sea to sea.
The Passion for us to set us free.

God Understands

Sharon Kaufman

Sometimes we face things we do not understand
and often forget that it is all in Gods hands.
He will allow certain situations for us to go through
but know in your heart that Jesus faced these things too.
We often feel like we go through this alone
but God is always with us to guide us safely home.
He understands these problems we face
that's why He offers us His love and grace.
He will be with us no matter how we feel
if we can remember that His love is very real.

Precious Lamb of God

Sharon Kemp

I am pursued by the most willful, deceitful, destructive enemy of all..."SELF". She wears her name proudly and boldly and stands with aggression glaring from her eyes. She is clothed with the armament of every temptation known to man, prepared for battle against my Shepherd for the prize He holds in His arms...me!

As I whirl in the barrage of her attacks, my squirming causes me to fall from my Shepherd's arms! As I am falling, I cry out in a desperate scream, "I don't want to become a captive of SELF!" and I am suddenly startled back into a realistic awareness. I feel the arms of my Shepherd catch me and wrap tightly around me. He bends His head forward to shield mine from the attack of SELF's arrows. With His mighty arm, He blocks the blows of her sword aimed for my heart. He takes the wounds intended for me and His blood flows over me. As I look upon my blood-covered body, I see letters being formed upon my heart. I feel strength and warmth return to my shivering, soaked body. As the last letter appears, I am overwhelmed with the compassion and offering that the written word reveals: "FORGIVEN".

SELF's defeat has been declared by the blood-wounds of my Shepherd's defensive stance (Isaiah 53:5). With my FORGIVEN heart, I snuggle in my Shepherd's arms and rest again upon His chest in serenity, security, and safety. In His arms my faith grows, my hope rests, and my love abounds (1 Corinthians 13). I am held in His grace and engulfed in His mercy. I am a precious lamb of God.

> Isaiah 40:11 - "He tends His flock like a shepherd: He gathers the lambs in His arms and carries them close to His heart." (NIV)

The Epitome of Self-Denial

Laura King

The Epitome of Self-Denial

Far gone from the kingdom whereof dwell
Seraphim's and
Cherub's.

To earth below to spare men's souls from
an endless state
of woe.

Thy vested kingly comforts shed,
no home nor bed,
instead.

With selfless care Thou didst forbear the
world and all of
its wares.

As the lowly poor Thou didst endure
this life without
grandeur.

Thou wast mocked and scourged and crucified,
for us Thou bled
and died.

No greater love Thou couldst impose to
redeem us from
sins throes.

As I quietly reflect on Thee,
in humbleness
I plead…

Pure gold is yet to be.
Hammer out the impurities found in me!

My cross is nigh awaiting,
yet I leave it where it stands.
Help me Lord to bear its sting,
nail it to my feeble hands.

For bound to it unfetters
selfishness that's wove within:
Just as Thou died for others
to release the bonds of sin.

> "If any man will come after me, let him deny himself, and take up his cross, and follow me. For whosoever will save his life shall lose it: and whosoever will lose his life for my sake shall find it." Matthew 16:24, 25 (Holy Bible, KJV).

Acquainted With Grief

Linda Kleinman

Shadows fell across the garden path as Jesus and the disciples entered the stillness of Gethsemane. Turning, Jesus looked on the three men. His voice shook with emotion, "My soul is exceedingly sorrowful unto death." Tears formed in his eyes as His face reflected deep distress. Reaching out he drew the men close, wrapping his arms around them in a tender embrace. Jesus leaned his head on Peter's shoulder as his body trembled from the pain of his grief. "Watch and pray that ye enter not into temptation." Walking a short distance he fell prostrate on the ground. Covering his face with his hands he groaned in agony. "Father, if it be possible, let this cup pass from me." The dreaded separation from his heavenly Father was unthinkable. Jesus' heart wrenched. His body, drenched in sweat, flooded the ground in pools. The spirit of evil filled the air as Satan whispered his lies. Crying aloud Jesus wept , fighting the pull of damnation, knowing he must enter that domain and possess the keys of Death and Hell. "Nevertheless, not my will but thine be done." Betrayed. Beaten and whipped beyond recognition as the flesh came off his back in sheets. Golgotha, where the nails violently pounded into his hands and feet caused blood to flow freely, covering Him. Crying out in agony as the Romans dropped the cross into a hole in the ground pulling bones out of joint. Suffocating as he tried to raise himself up to take a breath. Dying for Life. Life for you and me. Dying for Love. His love for us. Dying for our healing. Dying to bring you to heaven. Dying to live forevermore.

Not Just A Man

Thea Koeppen

He stands in front of the religiously zealot crowd watching the fervor that grips them. He blinks away sweat, thinking how mad the crowd is to be out today. They are dangerous, more so then proud people with swords. The powerful well-oiled chariot of the state crushes people with swords. A soldier can have pride in bringing the state glory. He turns, walking uphill. He knew glory in blood's sweet smell and the thrill of the fight for the right of Rome. He gazes up at the criminals.

The criminal in the center lifts his head. Their eyes meet. Was that compassion in the criminal's eyes? The soldier feels his chest tighten. Compassion FOR HIM! It pierces his heart and he feels shame. He wishes to look away, but can't. He swallows hard, fighting the sensation. A Roman Centurion never shows weakness.

Pain wracks the criminal's body, struggling, he cries out. His body jerks and his head hangs in death. The sky turns dark. The centurion's spine chills. A rumble and the ground shakes. He hears the crowd screaming, his soldiers trying to control them. Thunder booms, a sound reverberating in his soul. He feels sorrow engulf him. What has he done? His laughter as they shoved a thorn crown on the criminal's head, his voice shouting as they beat him with a cat-of-nine-tails, ripping flesh from bone. Crucified as a criminal. He had crucified this man? No, not just a man! What man could die so cruelly and have compassion on those inflicting his suffering? Deep inside a blazing fire, an answer.

Embracing courage he declares "Surely this man is the Son of God.

"A soldier calls. The Centurion starts away, glancing back. He had looked in the eyes of the Son of God and seen forgiveness.

No Passion Like His

Paulette Lackey

Passion a powerful feeling, the suffering of Christ after his death. There are some who felt anger and rage and there are toughs who were full of enthusiasm. Looking back to the death of Christ some may feel how could such a man lay down his life for all mankind.

He had taken on the sins of the world, a painful task but yet an act of passion and love. There is a scripture that states "will a man lay down his life for his friend?" In these last days we cannot fulfill the passion that Christ had and has for us .Man shall be lovers of self rather then lovers of God, another word for love is passion We can look at world news and see that it is basically an eye for and eye and a tooth for a tooth, some who are Christians are setting up what I call Mega Churches and not for the sake of the passion of Christ but for the material things they can get.

God in his compassionate way daily still says, "because of the Blood of my son you are forgiven." Note we all makes mistakes daily and we are forgiven. Christ cannot be placed back on the cross and because of his Love, Passion our sins are forever cast into the sea of forgetfulness. Look to the cross and you will see a man who died for you and me. Reflection on the cross has set us free, for all eternity, Come buy that which money cannot buy Isaiah 55:1.

Living For God

Wendy Lansford

Through all walks of life we make decisions and choices that affect both our present and our future. Decisions and choices that either promote, hinder or alter our walk with Jesus. At one point in time, the decisions and choices I made altered my walk with Christ; but now, those decisions have only enhanced it.

I have been completely focused this last year of my life on growing closer to God and abiding by his will for my life. To have a personal relationship with Jesus Christ is indescribable by words; you just have to experience it.

I have walked through many fires in my short 27 years of life; however, I would not be the woman I am today without having been through what I have been through. At this juncture in my life, one of the most important desires of my heart is growth and development. I want to grow and develop into the woman that God has planned and intended me to be. I want to do what he has called me to do. God has called me to openly share my testimony and to reach out to those in pain.

Our primary focus in life as believers is to win souls to the kingdom of God, to live life by following the example of Jesus Christ. My soul purpose is to follow God's will for my life; no decision is made (on my part) without thorough prayer and understanding of God's plan. The right decision is only right if it glorifies God.

What drove him to the Cross?

Doris Lawrence

What drove my Jesus to the cross that day?
Why didn't he just hide and run away?

He knew of the impending pain,
That they would nail him in his sides that day.

I'll tell you just what it was.
His love for the Father and because;

His passion was to be a pleasing son,
One that would submit and not turn and run.

He knew of his father's undying love,
For the creation that would be redeemed by his Son's blood.

Broken For You

Lisa Lollis

It was more than a ruthless way to die. More than unfair punishment to an innocent victim. More than a dramatic story to be portrayed and observed. More than the last breath of a life seemingly cut short. The Passion—the suffering of Jesus Christ. Yet His suffering was more than pain to His physical body. It was pain to the point of being broken. In 1 Corinthians 11:24, Jesus said to His disciples during their last meal, "...this is my body which is broken for you." Since John 19:36 proclaims that none of His bones were broken, what caused Jesus to use such a word? In simply looking at the Webster's Dictionary definition of "broken," our concept of Jesus' suffering deepens: "violated by transgression, made weak or infirm, subdued completely, cut off, disunited by divorce, separation or desertion of one parent." Was the suffering of Jesus physical? Yes. His body was human. However, those last few hours of our Savior represent the tremendous burden of our sins, sicknesses, fears. He bore so much weight of earthly transgression that Jesus cried out "My God, My God, why have you forsaken Me?" (Mark 15:34).

However, the suffering doesn't end in defeat! Before His death, Jesus took the cup and said, "This cup is the new covenant in My blood. This do, as often as you drink it, in remembrance of me." (1 Corinthians 11:25) In other words, Jesus was saying, "there is a greater purpose and power behind the suffering you will see with your natural eyes. I'm being broken so you can have new life." Simply receive and unwrap the gift of the new life in Christ Jesus. Don't let the passion, the suffering of Christ be in vain. He was broken for you!

Sweetest Name Indeed

Roland Marke

When I sing a tune music flows within
Soothing music peace like a current
Name above others so worthy to adore
Powerful blend of love, joy and peace
Miraculous power authority revolves.

Satan quits when you sound His name
Offers freedom, justice and compassion
Christians claim your legal rights please
Souls do what it takes to become saved
Only believers thrive evoking His name
Saints claim anything evoking His name

Why miss tremendous endless blessings
Try His name in faith to prove the truth
Claim your desires ambition every need
In patience faith hope you will receive
Name above all others power so mighty
A name so sacred His name is "JESUS"

I am Worth His Cause

Victoria Masters

We all have a story to tell. We can each glean a sense of inspiration someone's story. I share this story in hope that someone will know his or her worth because of Christ.

As a child, I always knew there was a God. My father was a preacher, yet I thought of God as someone waiting to strike me dead if I did something wrong. I viewed Him as I viewed my parents—if I did something wrong, either parent was there to verbally assault me. As I grew into this world I grew passionless, waiting for someone else to define my life. I never knew who I was; let alone what I meant to Christ.

So, the man I married was a physical and emotional terror. I believed that since I made the choice to marry Him, I would have to live with that choice. There was no purpose for my life. My skin was gray, I was slowly dying, my hair was falling out, and I was young. Still something in my soul stirred, I was searching for truth.

It was an epiphany when I discovered that God chose me to be His own. The Son of the living God was sacrificed for me, and Christ became my all. I left the marriage. If God, knowing all my sins, loves me and died for me, then who is man to treat me any less?

Christ has a passion for His people. It is the reason he was crucified. I believe he has placed a desire for Him in the depth of every human. If we chase after His goodness with our every being, He will reveal to us our true self-worth and purpose. It is us then who will have that same passion for only Him.

A Night In The Kings Presence

Ruthe McDonald

What if you could swallow the moon and have its light just illuminate from within? Beams of light just shining through every pore of your body. Wouldn't that be amazing? Well, that is exactly how I felt after spending a night in Jesus' presence.

I was feeling discouraged and depressed. Everything in my life just seemed to be going the wrong way. I've been serving the Lord since I was seven, I am now thirty-two. Sometimes as we get older, we forget just how awesome God really is. Because, everything just seems so much simpler when you're younger. As we get older, sometimes instead of getting wiser, we get forgetful. Forgetting to take delight in the wonders of our Lord and Savior, and the gift he gave us.

As a child, I was fascinated with the moon and stars. I would talk to the moon and the stars...and they spoke back! That is how God communicated with my spirit. One night, I looked out the window, after feeling so discouraged and heartbroken and I noticed how bright the moon was and the many stars that were out. I begin to speak to them again. Forgetting how old I was or that I may seem silly. I didn't care. I needed to spend some time in the King's presence. I spoke him, and He said to me, "I'm the same God that spoke to you then. I'm with you all the time. I've never left you, or forgotten you. I love you and always will. Rest in me. Remember, I came just for you."

Tears just flowed down my face. The passion that God has for His children. To die on the cross for me, so that I might live. To rise again, so that I may be free. To love me, even when I didn't love myself. It's good to spend the night in the King's presence. You might just remember some things long forgotten and drink in the presence of his light.

The Truth

Chad Meriwether

This is who I am
and all that I am not
This is what I offer
its everything I've got
I give you my life
Take control of me
I die unto myself
so You can set me free
its the least that I can do
after all that you have done
for you love me so much
that you sent your only son
He walked this earth for me
and felt my very pain
He kept His head held high
even while they mocked His name
He cared for every soul
knowing some would turn
He reached out to them all
so none would have to burn
He only spoke the truth
so everyone could know
He told them all to listen
so they knew which way to go
He looked beyond their eyes
and saw directly in their heart
He put together the pieces
of a world that fell apart
He didn't care about status
or how many friends He had

He focused on His job
and not the latest fad
He only came to earth
to fulfill His fathers plan
this would be His job
die, to save every man
and now I must confess
it was I who drove the nail
I put Him on that cross
I sent my God to hell
I made the crown of thorns
I place it on His head
I stood there in the crowd
and did nothing while He bled
I shoved the spear in His side
I saw it cut through the skin
but blood did not flow down
instead it was my every sin
I hung next to Him on the cross
all covered in blood and shame
I realized that I'm a sinner
and I shouted out His name
He turned and looked at me
I couldn't look Him in the eye
"truly you shall be with Me"
He said looking to the sky.

A Rugged Piece of Wood

Sheila Mitchell

Mount Calvary Trembled
As it resounded with the echo of His cry;
Cruel hatred pierced his side,
Offering no compassion.

The jeering crown looked on to see
If the Son of God would bow his knee
And retreat from this painful death.
It could not understand.

"It is finished", He proclaimed,
And died with dignity.

A rugged piece of wood,
Gloriously transformed,
A symbol of hope
For all mankind.

My Cry of Forgiveness

Diane Nolan

I woke up with tears flowing down my face. My head bowed down in awe that Christ died for me.

I was dreaming. I was clutching the cross where Jesus is and was crucified. The sky was the most awesome orange and rose sunset and through my tears and long hair I could see the outline of the landscape as I was hanging onto the cross. As my heart ached, my voice rang out into the barren surroundings of Calvary. From the depths of my soul I was crying out, "Father Forgive them, for they know not what they do." I can feel every splinter penetrate my hands as my body crumbles to the foot of the cross weeping. I look up at Our Lord Jesus on the cross while tears were streaming down my face, my body broken and weary.

Jesus came down from the cross. He knelt down, and with tears streaming down My Savior's face; He picked me up into His arms. He began to walk down the hill of Calvary. I was physically standing at the base of the cross watching Jesus carry me down the hill. I was resting in the arms of Christ.

There was only one set of footprints. When Christ died, He died for all sinners. When He rose He saved us from the world. For those that are called are not of the world. Jesus said to the disciples, "Go into all the world and preach the good news to all creation." Mark 16:15

Matthew 11:28—"Come to me all you who are weary and burdened, and I will give you rest."

Mark 12:30—"Love the Lord thy God with all your heart, and with all your soul, and with all your mind, and with all your strength: this is the first and most important commandment."

My dream November 29, 2003.
Scripture taken from NIV Zondervan Study Bible.

My Good Shepherd (John 16)

Sarah Nordlund

Jesus, my Good Shepherd, calls me by my name
and when I hear His voice, my life no longer is the same.

For my Good Shepherd will always protect and provide
all He asks me to do is stay close to His side.
He must go before me and prepare the way,
smoothing out rough spots or driving evil away.

Gently He pulls with His staff made of wood
all those wandering lambs who are self-seeking their food.
He alone provides for all His flocks' needs;
giving shelter, food, and providing safe sleep.

At the end of each day as I enter the fold
He lowers His rod and under it I must go.
By this He examines me intently from head to feet
in search of any wounds that He could lovingly treat.

Oh grateful I'm just a lamb, who must follow not lead,
that I have a Good Shepherd who loves me indeed!
Who calls me by name,
Who heals all my wounds
Who feeds me, protects me,
Jesus Christ I love you....my Good Shepherd.

The Passivity of the Passion

Rev. F. Marshall North

The crucifixion of Jesus Christ is to me a clear statement against revenge. As a Christian, I believe Jesus to have been God incarnate—the creator of the universe. I no more comprehend the immensity of His power than I can the expansiveness of the universe. I cannot even begin to analogize the depth of His love.

In human terms, He subjected Himself to great pain at the hands of His persecutors and in human terms, He experienced that pain. Those who profess Him to be the Son of God must believe as well that He at anytime during His torture could have wreaked havoc upon His would be killers. Yet, He did not. He endured the pain and suffering as a means to a greater end the—salvation of mankind.

Had He have struck back on that day, what proof would we have of eternal life? He would have been no better than those who sought to rid their lives of Him. In the Passion of Christ we can see ourselves in those times we feel beaten, ridiculed, failed, rejected and want to strike back to get even. An "eye for an eye" as it was. Christ shows us that our depleted state is only temporary. Through Him and His Gospel we will one day realize an eternity of unsurpassed joy. He gives us hope. Revenge is indeed its own reward whether against a person or a nation. Whatever the gain is will be savored only a short while.

The Passion of Christ directs us to what lies beyond retaliation. In obedience to His example and sacrifice, rather than a temporal and pseudo satisfaction, we will realize eternal JOY.

O What Love?

Unuigbe Ohi

✠

Isn't it insatiable hunger for the
salvation of man's lost soul
The driving force behind
Christ's ministerial goal?
Sweet Jesus! Compassionate
son of a "terrible" father
Begotten to demonstrate to man
that man's neighbors is his brother,
He chose to be born
in a stable—a place so lowly,
So He can have access to the majority of
ordinary folks who are meek , simple and lovely.
His invaluable love exceeds
the boundaries of man's spiritual affairs-
For, isn't His maiden miracle in Cana of Galilee
a demonstration of His care for man's welfare?
He restored blind peoples, sight,
and made fowl spirits right...
Bosom full of love—Jesus Christ,
The way, the truth and the light...
Propelled by love, He went all about preaching salvation,
With a loaf and two fish,
He arrested five thousand peoples' starvation.
Consumed by anger at the corruption of
God's temple, He overturned the Money Changer's table
But with his friends he there endured a relationship that was stable—
He resisted the Pharisees
And Sadducees entertaining no fear...

Only openly proclaiming God's love…
This good news, the world must hear.
From one whose feet He washed,
He got a better kiss of betrayal;
And in Gethsemane Garden,
He felt the disappointment of a turned down prayer.
He was arrested, falsely found guilty,
And with a whip his flesh was torn;
Scornful Roman soldiers honoured Him with a Coronation of Thorns—
They nailed Him like
A common criminal to the Cross,
What shame! Intending His
Grievous death to be a loss;
He bled and suffered
Pain as his throat dried,
From the heavy burden of
Mankind's sin on his shoulders, He cried…
O, what love moved Him
To pray for the forgiveness of murderous man,
As on the Cross painfully He died
To fulfill God's grand plan.
He rose up on the third day
And over death he is boss…
But O such love that can never let go,
Christ sent the Holy Ghost to come
Reside in Man's heart and make it His home

Reflections on the Passion of Jesus

Yvonne Paramore

Jesus was passionate about the message and the mission given Him by our Heavenly Father. Jesus' message was the Word of God; His mission was to suffer and die on the cross. Jesus did not speak of His own accord but spoke only what His Father wanted Him to say, in the way the Father wanted him to say it. Because Jesus accomplished His mission, dying on the cross, believers have salvation and spend eternity with the Father and the Son.

Jesus, as the Word, was the passionate expression of God's love. The many parables Jesus used in explaining the Father's love, mercy, forgiveness, and the heavenly Kingdom, shows Jesus' passion for proclaiming the Word. Jesus wanted the disciples to know, understand, believe, and teach, others what he knew to be true about His Heavenly Father and the heavenly Kingdom. To teach the truth of salvation, Jesus taught lovingly and passionately through the parables.

Jesus' passion was produced by His life's purpose and reason for being; to show that a sinful and broken world could be healed and restored in God's grace. Jesus healed the physically and spiritually sick. Jesus healed the physically ill through their faith, for it was by their faith that they were made whole, able to pick-up their mat and walk, and were forgiven of their sins. The passionate and saving words of Jesus brought healing to a world that was spiritually ailing.

Finally, Jesus accomplished His mission on earth as a passionate love offering for the salvation of believers. Through the body, blood, passion and love of Jesus, a new covenant was established for all time with all mankind. We are saved because Jesus was passionate about the message and mission given Him by our Heavenly Father.

Others

Jeffrey Paul

Unable to bear the cross, Jesus fell to the ground. A man coming in from North Africa was pressed into service to carry the cross behind Jesus. They arrived at the hill called "the place of the skull"—Golgotha in Hebrew Aramaic, Calvary in Latin. Pilate sent along a sign to be placed on the cross—"Jesus the Nazarene, The King of the Jews," written in Greek, Latin, and the local Hebrew Aramaic, so passers-by could know who was being crucified.

After He rejected the medicated wine, the soldiers crucified Him naked and lifted Him up from the earth in front of the multitudes, the beloved John, the religious leaders, His mother, and the women. He was openly shamed. We might expect that with the pain and disgrace He would have been too distraught to take notice of others. At this horrible point at the end of His life we could not expect Him to be "others minded." Yet His unpredictable moments show that His mind was not on Himself.

He asked Father to forgive those who had driven nails through His body. In doing so He rebuked the world's love of vengeance. He assured a contrite thief hanging next to Him that, "today you shall be with Me in Paradise." Then, as oldest son, He tenderly saw to the care of His mother. Looking down from the cross, "Woman, Behold, your son." To the beloved John, "Behold your mother." How very precious that these words were recorded for us!

He was anything but precious to those who cursed Him. His enemies spoke hatred without interruption. Looking upon the crucified, they scoffed out a tremendous truth: "He saved others; He cannot save Himself" How true! He could not save Himself from death if He would bring life to the world.

His Loneliness

Jason Powers

Loneliness is in a class that nobody wants to fit in, but the sad part about it is that so many have experienced this thing called loneliness. Maybe for you loneliness is a part of life, the lonely nights by yourself. The days you feel all alone having no one to talk to. You wonder, will this feeling of loneliness ever end. It feels like everyone has forsaken you. Well, I know a person who experienced loneliness at a level we will never have to face. This person is Jesus Christ who paid such a price for all man kind on the cross. He suffered loneliness in a way that would break any ordinary person. But Jesus looked at the eternal reward instead of the temporary pain and loneliness. Imagine being betrayed by your friend who was so close to you. Judas Iscariot was the friend who betrayed Jesus the Son of God. The agony Jesus must have felt. Soon after the great multitude with swords and staves took Jesus His very own disciples forsook Him, leaving Jesus all alone with His enemies in the garden of Gethsemane. The feeling of loneliness must have been great upon the Lord. I can't imagine what that level of loneliness must have been like, but I am sure thankful that Jesus was willing to pay that price for us. By the time Jesus was taken to the cross He was so warn out from the torture and pain that on the cross He cried out "My God, My God why hast thou forsaken me?" Never have words express such loneliness before. This was the price Jesus was willing to pay so you and I would never have to feel all alone all the days of our lives.

I Did It For You

Carlene Ramsey

Dear Loved One,

You watched me come into this world
I did it for you
You watched me grow up into a wise young man
I did it for you
You saw me give wisdom, knowledge and understanding to the ignorant
I did it for you
You saw me give healing, peace, and life
I did it for you
You watched as they criticized and rejected me
I did it for you
You watched them as they took me to trial and found me guilty of nothing
I did it for you
I never said a word as the beat me unrecognizably
I did it for you
I never said a word as they ripped my skin to shreds and put thorns on my head
I did it for you
I never said a word as they put nails in my main veins so I can bleed to death
I did it for you
I could have said no when I walked down that path the Calvary, but I cared so much for
your soul
I did it for you

As I bled and hung on the cross, I thought about your future and what it holds
I did it for you
I could have got down and said I will not, but I loved you so
I did it for you
Now that the future is here and yet you still reject me, I still love you and I am still
doing it just for you.

Your Number One Love,
Jesus Christ

Just Another Friday?

Jason Retherford

Today is Good Friday. Good, hmm, stark irony to a Friday long ago. An angry mob. Mock trials and mockery. Beatings after beatings. Bruises and blood stained skin. The bloodthirsty crowd wanted him dead, and now. But why, what crime did he commit?

Well none. His death sentence may be the greatest mockery of justice ever. Isaiah said that the Messiah would be numbered with the transgressors (Is. 53:12). Those that gripped the tightest the doctrine of God's law claimed that this man, this Galilean blasphemed God by claiming to be a king, by claming to be the Son of God. But not once during his whole life did his words contradict the words of the Father. Not once did he raise his hand to strike a brother. Not once did he covet what he did not have. No, the One who stood before Pilate is the One who has stood in the hallways of Heaven in the presence of the Father. The hands that were bound were the ones that touched the untouchables. His words spoke of the promise of life, but now the words of his accusers were those that would lead to his death.

The verdict was pronounced, and now the Author of Life was marched to meet Death. The walk from Pilate's palace to hill of Golgotha would be a death march. A few days prior, throngs of people lined the streets of Jerusalem to welcome Jesus, to welcome the Messiah. They sang Hosannas, now they hurled hate-filled words at the One from Heaven. Yet He marched on. He knew His mission, and He knew His Father was watching. Reaching Golgotha, the Roman soldiers executed their orders and they executed the carpenter from Nazareth. It was hear at the place of the skull (Golgotha), that the Bread of Life was broken. Innocent, the Lamb of God was slaughtered.

Oh the pain He endured! Oh, the wretched pain.

The pain of betrayal.
Hours earlier a disciple's kiss lead to His arrest.
His friends, His closest companions fled into the night.
The people who once praised Him, now cursed Him.

The pain of death.
Nails ripping through flesh.
Bruises from beatings.
Scars from scourging.
A crown of thorns ripping through His forehead.
The mind numbing agony of crucifixion,
And the horror of grasping for each breath

He endured the pain of sin.
Every thoughtless word.
Every selfish deed.
Every hand raised in anger to strike another.
Every sin from The Garden of Eden to Golgotha to you and me.

He endured the pain of separation.
For all eternity the Father and the Son had enjoyed constant unity.
With the sky blackening, the Father looked away.
Any wonder the cry from the cross. "My God, My God why have you forsaken me."
Jesus died alone, soaked with our sins, and soaked with His own blood

What will you do with this Friday. A Friday that is unlike any other. Will you run and flee like His closest companions or will stay near the cross like a few of his followers whose love for this man brought them near even in the face of death. Choose to spend time near the cross. Reflect on this man's life. His words, His love,

His compassion. His death though tragic, leads us to follow Him still. Follow Him beyond Friday. You're in for a treat. Amen.

Gratefully His,
Jason M. Retherford

Will Of the Father

Velma Roberts

The Will of the Father
forms the very essence of my being.
I gladly lay down My Life to redeem all who are lost.
I Am the Last Adam that will reunite mankind to their Lord God Creator.
It is this mission that drives Me
to My knees
to the cross of My Death
to My Resurrection.
For this Purpose-
The Will Of The Father
that I live
that I die
that I live
that I reign.

Our Tears Were Mingled Together

Sandra Ruoff

I saw him again today. He was carrying a cross, dragging it through town. The blood stained robe and that horrible mockery of a crown made of thorns. Why the humiliation? I remember the first time I met him. I was caught with another woman's husband in town. The men all dragged me out to the gate to stone me. I know I deserved that, after all I was the town harlot and our law said that anyone caught doing that must die. He said something to the men that made them all look down in shame and one by one they walked away. I thought he would throw the stones himself, but instead he told me I was forgiven and to stop my harlotry. I loved him for that great act of kindness. Whenever I saw him after that he was always helping someone. I heard he even could raise the dead! I never knew for sure if that was true, but that didn't matter to me. He gave me back my dignity. That meant everything to me. But today he looked so heavy, like he was carrying the weight of the whole world. They nailed him to the cross he had carried. He looked so out of place there beside those two men. They were deserving of that punishment. Our eyes met, that Nazarenes and mine. I was so confused and weeping uncontrollably. He was crying out too. I felt somehow that our tears were mingled together. Mine were tears of regret, his were of love and anguish. He said "Paid in full!" I thought about those words on the long walk back to where I live. I think I'll be pondering those words for the rest of my life.

Lama Sabachthani

Jean-Ann Semple

Away with him! Crucify him!
And thus it was.
The women did wail. The women did mourn
As that cross he'd stumblingly borne.

So darkness lay upon the land
And all creation waited.
The wind it was still
And the trees stood sentinel.

The sins of souls were gathering
Spanning time and spanning space.
Stored sins and griefs from since the fall
Upon Him lay the iniquities of all.

"Eloi! Eloi! Lama sabachthani!"
Forsaken by God
Despised and rejected by men
He gave up the ghost and died.

The earth did quake and
The rocks did split
And the graves
They opened wide.

And the people drew near
And the soldiers did fear
For their doubts they'd denied
Of this man they'd crucified.

"We did it! We did it!" the devil cried
And he chortled gleefully
"He's dead. He's dead" his cohorts said
And they commenced to spree.

But who is this come striding in
Breathing fire in pillared smoke
Sacrificed garments dipped in blood
Dropping sweet-smelling myrrh?

It's the Lamb! It's the Lamb!
It's the one they crucified
See His hands. See His feet
See His brow where all sorrows meet!

And the demons they started
The imps they fell back.
The evil one saw his doom,
And his jaw, it fell slack.

Tiers and tiers of wicked ones
Rows and rows of them
Vanquished and beaten they did turn
Gibbering and quivering they fled.

Oh Look upon the One that now emerges
The victor's smile upon His face
He's clothed in glory; He's full of grace
He was burnt with frankincense.

The Lion of the tribe of Judah
The root of Jesse's stem, He hath prevailed.
And in His hands He holds aloft
The keys of death and hell.

Black and Blue — The Colors of Love

Flora Seward

Jesus died on the cross of Calvary for you and for me. Black and blue are the colors of His wounds that He suffered for you and for me the day that He died. God the Father is love. Jesus the son is love also. He loved us so very much that he was willing to suffer a horrible death. He was beaten unrecognizable. He took all the pain, suffering, sickness, and disease that we would ever experience in our lives into His own body that day on Calvary. Jesus said in the Book of John that His kingdom is not of this world. When He died on Calvary He understood what was happening to Him and He knew that it was going to happen. His disciples did not understand and they turned their backs on Him and left Him to this horrible death, but Jesus being the savior that He is laid down His life willing for you and for me. I am so glad that He did. I am free because of His redemptive work at Calvary. Jesus, I could never thank you enough for what You did for me. I know that You love me and I love You, too.

Easter

Tyrone Short

"I have seen the Lord, I have seen the Lord"
These are the words of Mary Magdalene
The shocking revelation of these words
Is that refer to the sighting of the dead Nazarene
He said that he will back
But not one took it serious
Especially after seeing his crucifixion
Which had left him lifeless

A miracle such as this couldn't have been done by just a prophet
Because he did more than just take God's words and interpret
A miracle such as this couldn't have been done by just a rabbi
Because no other ordained leader could resurrect after they die

This is why we celebrate Easter
And hold onto our faith in the risen Christ
He said "Peace be with us"
Until he comes back, which will be twice

The first time will be for the church which we call the rapture
The second time with the army of Heaven to rule with an iron scepter
Blessed are those who have not seen, and yet they still believe
Woe to those who deny the truth, for eternity their soul will grieve

Passion

Gertude Slaback

✠

P urposely,
A
S avior
S teps
I nto
O ur
N ight

The Savior's Plea

Candice Smith

Dear child of God, I already bore the unbearable heaviness of your sorrow, don't wait to give it up until the arrival of another tomorrow.

Our Father never created you to persistently bear such great burdens and pain, if you would just give your heartbreak to me total peace would be yours to gain.

I desire above all that you understand the truth, my love for you is so infinitely great and I have proved it's true, even when you shunned our Father, I gave up my life to seal your eternal fate.

Accept my free gift to you, for total restoration in eternal salvation and then freely give as I gave to you, by spreading my love to the upcoming generation.

If it is your confession that you invited me inside, don't ever allow doubt to cause my power within you to hide.

With the Holy Spirit be baptized with fire, do as I have done and I promise you will never tire.

Jesus Came to Raise the Dead

Karla Stai

The year was 1994, the month of April. As a family we were taking the educational trip of a lifetime. Traveling by way of train, we spent three days crossing the United States enjoying God's beauty, getting off at our various national cities of great importance. We stopped to spend a week with my parents in Florida before boarding the train once again for another weeks worth of learning and adventure. Our next stop was Washington D.C. for two days. As we left my parents, our youngest daughter, Elizabeth, who was two at the time, began to show flu-like symptoms. We were unable to change our trip agenda or train fares for others, so we prayed and left believing the God would heal her. For two solid days on the train, our little girl was so ill that nothing would stay in her stomach. Wrenching and tossing and turning for hours on end. We tried everything. To make matters worse, ALL the restrooms on the train had "suddenly" gotten plugged. Vomiting and diarrhea into plugged unflushable toilets for two days! I was pregnant with child number five and wasn't feeling so well myself. By the time we came into Washington D.C., our little angel had collapsed, couldn't talk, walk, sit or respond to us. As a mom, I emotionally freaked out. Subway after subway, finally a taxi ride to the emergency room. The doctor in charge checked Elizabeth over and said that her tiny veins had collapsed from dehydration and that we should put her into the hospital. He couldn't even find a vein to put an I.V. in. Things were bad. Then and there we had to make a decision to allow my husband to take all the kids back to Minnesota and leave a pregnant, emotionally spent wife with our daughter thousands of miles from home or to trust God and take her home-knowing the results were poor at best. After praying all night for God to heal her and not seeing any progress, I didn't want to proceed anywhere. I was ready to camp and wait for the doctors to do their stuff. At last the doctor said, you know, we really can't do much for her...why don't you head home and plan to have her airlifted closer to home. We agree and as we left, the doctor touched her head and Elizabeth responded. She began pointing to a purple sucker...after not eating for almost a week now...hmm. We gave her the sucker and it stayed down. Finally a parched, bleeding mouth was moist. To make a very long story shorter, we spent the next day in D.C. and boarded the train for home. Elizabeth was doing no better so we made arrangements to get off the train earlier and get home. As I lay with my hand on her rising and falling rapid breathes and wildly beating heart, I continued to pray until I fell into exhausted sleep. I then was suddenly awakened by our little 16 pound two-year-old standing on the floor tugging at my shirt. "Mommy, mommy, I want something to eat!" I turned to look at a sickly girl with black circles under her eyes and ribs protruding. I saw a picture of health smiling at me. Elizabeth said, "Mommy, Jesus was here. He stood at the foot of my bed and then came over and kissed me right here (on the forehead) He told me He loved me and I was healed!" "Now get up I want to eat!" Jesus once again, in His own timing, came down to earth and had passion for a little girl, that he raised her from the dead! We are so truly thankful!

He Did It All

Lisa Y. Sullivan

They pierced His hands, side, and feet.
His blood ran that eternal death you and I not meet.
They mocked and scorned him as he hung on the cross.
He endured it all that you and I not live lost.
They placed him in a tomb, and thought he was done.
He rose on the third day with all power, and the victory over death won.
He did it all for the remission of our sins.
He restored us to the Father for only he could make amends.
Yes, he brought the kingdom of heaven to you and me.
This gift of true life is yours to receive if in Christ Jesus you believe.

Passion From the Cross

Michele Sutphin

A Golden night I lay down to dream,
prayers on my lips and in my heart,
kneeling at the foot of a piece of wood,
my hands clinging to it,
wondering why I should,
the smells and sounds came with blood
streaming down my hands,
looking up I then did understand,
words could not come from loss,
I knew I held onto the rugged cross,
my head I lifted with tears streaming down,
to see my Savior this way,
so long ago Him, I had found,
to see the spikes through hands and feet,
His loving sacrifice for so many sins,
that I could be redeemed and not know defeat,
my heart so raced with love I had never known,
that I realized that on that cross,
this Lamb of God,
for me suffered alone,
such passion , such power He had showed me
then I realized what Jesus Christ wanted from me,
to share this passion , His love to everyone, everywhere,
so they too would know what He did on that cross,
that for each heart, He cares.

The Rose

Diana Taylor

With velvet petals folded back,
To catch the morning dew,
It spread its fragrant glory
Through the daybreak's golden hue.
Reaching out, I sought to grasp
Its beauty for my own,
But with a cry of pain drew back,
And left the rose alone.
Wanting just to pluck its bloom,
I'd grasped a hidden thorn,
And from my careless wounding
Crimson touched the rose that morn.
For beauty bears a burden,
And attainment comes with pain.
Our life, the cost to know the Rose
That bore the crimson stain.
A gentle Rose that slowly walked
Golgotha's dusty vale,
His beauty marred by cruel thorns,
His visage scarred and pale.
Down from the stripes and crown He wore,
Trailed life-blood in the dust,
A wounded Rose and still to bear
The cruel blade's final thrust.
A wilted flower bent His head
On Calvary's silent crest,
And lovingly, in Joseph's tomb
Was gently laid to rest.

Yet on that glorious morning,
In the coolness of the dawn,
The Rose of Sharon bloomed anew,
With pain and sorrow gone.
Bruised for our iniquity and wounded for our sin,
He bloomed that Heaven's glory
Might be ours to enter in.

Salvation

Daniel Vaughn

Before this wind and rain to come
to take me down below the sea,
I try to stop the boats succumb,
I myself, together me.

Rain I catch with hands together,
weathered waves of violent motion,
and between fingers fragile grasp,
it leaks and falls into the ocean.

Faith forgotten, screaming plead,
but out from in a voice then calms,
with eyes, into my hands, cast down,
His face stares out from in my palms.

Revive, I pray, me from this prison
to survive in Your embrace.
Within Your grasp, within Your touch,
into my hands my buried face.

Lift the burdened years I carry,
hold my hand, Lord, it is wary.
Take me far above the sea,
I with You, together we.

Distant Love

Barbara Villarreal

Away in a manger it did begin
Love for You comes from within

Our life prior to mine
Your loving care ever so kind

Your tranquility gets me through the day
Graciously forgiving the folly I play

Every activity handled differently
in a daily walk with You spiritually and physically

Though not one in the flesh
Spiritually we mesh.

Our love appears distant at times
When together my Spirit chimes.

Though not here in body I sense Your wondrous splendor
This makes me feel so pleasantly tender

Oh, my distant love
Taking care to see me from above

Getting closer to me as I allow
Born long ago yet here and now

Though distant at times we seem to be
Ever the need Your love for me.

No matter how close or distant it can be
My love for You, Your love for me

A Simple Revelation of the Blood

Charles Waddell

As I sit here in silence, thinking about the revelation that has been shown to me about the Blood of Jesus I realize the simplicity of it all. The blood that was shed on Calvary was shed because He loved us. Not because we were worthy, but simply because we are loved. Because of that simple act of love we can look back on the cross with assurance and say, "I am special, I am never alone, somebody loves me." Never again do you have to look at your life in the eyes of depression. Why?

Because on a simple cross, someone showed you love. Because of its simplicity, the cross gives victory over life's complexities. The love that was shown to us on the cross gives us a reason to live, a reason to carry on. If we can ever grasp the concept that the God that created us loves us so much that He sent His son Jesus to die on that cross we will change the world. No longer will we live defeated lives, no longer will we allow the enemy to attack our families, no longer will we NOT live in victory, if we will simply understand the simplicity that lies in the love and the blood of the cross.

No Greater Love

Candi Ware

My morning started off with a spirit of complaining, due to the lack of sleep from the night before. I complained from the time I woke till it was time for me to leave for work. I dropped my daughters off at day care and continue to complain some more. At the half way point to my job a spirit of conviction came upon me. Immediately the way I acted flashed before my eyes.

Taken on a spiritual journey to a time when a man was sent to walk the face of the earth. Rejected, betrayed with a kiss, spit at, beaten and mocked. Crucified so, that our sin could be forgiven. As the mockers chanted crucify him! He looked down on those same individuals speaking these very words. "Father Forgive them for they know not what they do."

I could visualize the blood streaming from his side, the lashes across his back. A crown of thorns crushed down on his head. I often wondered why I was taken back to reflect on his suffering. Jesus wanted me to realize that he died on the cross for me and never once complained. He was laid to rest only to rise three days later, victoriously to prove to the world that Satan had been defeated.

There is no greater love.

His Love

Destiny Warwick

Sometimes I wonder if Jesus Christ knew
When he was little, what he'd grow up to do
Did he know that he'd die for all of his friends?
And people he didn't even know, then come back again?
And I wonder if the Man who saved my life
Would like peanut butter or pizza, would he fly a kite?
Did he have any pets, like a cat or a dog?
Did he ever come home and show mom a frog?
I wonder sometimes if he'd like what I like
Would he go to the movies; would he ride a bike?
Did he know about TV, and if he did, did he tell?
Or did he keep it secret so we'd find out ourselves?
But there are times when I realize he was just like me:
Just a normal kid, but with power to set people free.
And that's why he did it. That's why he died.
So that we could ask questions about Jesus' life.

Dialogue of a Father and a Son

R. Dale Watkins

Let us take a walk through time from Heaven's view:

"Then God said, 'Let us make man in our image, in our likeness, and let them rule over the fish of the sea and the birds of the air, over the livestock, over all the earth, and over all the creatures that move along the ground.'" It had begun.

A comprehensive decision. A unanimous vote to decide to bring life to man that God may love him. When he chose death, God, the Most High, lost his most precious creation. Much like losing a friend, a masterpiece, a diamond, a son.

There is no record of their next conversation.

The Christ, the Only Begotten of God, came to earth and walked amongst the scorned.

"As soon as Jesus was baptized, he went up out of the water. At that moment heaven was opened, and he saw the Spirit of God descending like a dove and lightning on him. And a voice from heaven said, "This is my Son, whom I love, with him I am well pleased." It was decided.

"Father, if you are willing, take this cup from me; yet not my will, but yours be done." It was yielded.

"Father, the time has come. Glorify your Son, that your Son may glorify you. Father, just as you are in me and I am in you. May they also be in us. Righteous Father. I know you. and made you known that the love you have for me may be in them and that I myself may be in them." It was time.

"Eloi, Eloi, lama sabachthani—My God, my God, why have you forsaken me?"

"It is finished!"

Risen - Ascended - Enthroned.

"Behold, I am coming soon! My reward is with me."

Come, Lord Jesus, come!

Wounded Healer

Stuart Wood

By your stripes we are healed;
The ultimate plan through death revealed.
A total failure many thought.
Naked, exposed, our freedom bought.

Shame and ridicule, joke and jibe
From leaders of the religious tribe.
Though beaten and broken, barely alive,
Your only words were "Father, forgive."

Wounds inflicted through fear and pride,
Deceit and hypocrisy deep inside
Those men of God, who knew the rules,
But not your love; they were the fools!

All man's sin on you was laid,
Demons shouted as our price you paid.
Jeering and mocking, then anxious doubt
As Satan's worst became your victory shout.

So why do we continue to blame
Our fellow believers and heap on shame
When they fail and fall, and are broken too?
No chance to be healers, or to follow you.

From brokenness comes healing, from forgiveness, fire.
Rebuilding and equipping, a burning desire
To bring life to the dying and direction to the lost.
Because we're all sinners bought at equal cost!

Copyright © 2004 Stuart Wood (through Waywood Music)

Jesus Does Answer Prayer

JoAnne Wright

"Mommy, Mommy, help!" Into the house ran four years old, Tammy. Tears running down her face.

"There's a beautiful flower outside, and I can't pick it for you. There's a great big bee on it, and he might sting me."

"Well," replied Mommy. "Did you pray to Jesus about it?"

Hanging her head, Tammy said, " I never thought about that. Jesus doesn't care about a little flower, does He?"

Mommy knelt down, gently cupped her little girls chin in her hand. "Oh, yes dear. Jesus cares about every thing. Even your flower. He sees your tears, and He loves you."

Tammy's eyes opened up in excitement. "Oh, Mommy, can we pray now? Please Mom, can we?"

Very lovingly, Mommy said, "Of course we can dear."

Right there in the open door, Tammy and Mommy knelt to pray. Mommy prayed first. "Dear Jesus, I am so glad that you love my little girl. She has a very special place in mine and your hearts. I thank you for listening to her, and answering her prayer."

Then Tammy prayed, "Hi Jesus. Please take the bee away so I can pick the beautiful flower for my Mommy. Thank you Jesus. I love you."

Tammy ran outside. Very soon after that, in came a very excited little girl. "Mommy, Mommy, the bee is gone!" Her face just beamed as she handed her Mommy a big beautiful Dandelion. Then with a kiss, she whispered, "Jesus does answer prayer."

The Love of Christ

Forrest Wychopen

What kind of love is this? That Jesus Christ, the very essence and expression of God, would die for me. Oh the depth of His love! So unconditional. So undeserved. So complete.

I do not fully comprehend His passion, yet, with childlike faith, I receive His atonement in full-I accept His love which is manifested in Christ. "And you, that were sometime alienated and enemies in your mind by wicked works, yet now hath he reconciled. In the body of his flesh through death, to present you holy and unblameable and unreproveable in his sight" (Colossians 1:22).

Why do I love Him? Is it because my mind recalls the good things He has done? Do I love Him because He commands me to do so? Apart from Him, I am incapable of loving. Apart from Jesus Christ, I have no desire to love. I love Him because He first loved me. God was the initiator. Righteous God pursued sinful me. And by faith in Jesus Christ alone, the love of God is now shed abroad in my heart! I have a new heart. A new life. Abundant and free.

The passion of Christ gives me purpose. The passion of Christ has made me pure. What immeasurable love is this? "For he hath made him to be sin for us, who knew no sin; that we might be made the righteousness of God in him. (2 Corinthians 5:21)

Would such a gift as this be ignored? No! The passion of Christ constrains us to follow Him. For we are His workmanship, His creation-created in Christ Jesus unto good works." And now, little children, abide in him; that, when he shall appear, we may have confidence, and not be ashamed before him at his coming." (1 John 2:28)

Jesus Is Free

Virginia Young

Jesus love is whole and free
It doesn't cost a thing you see
Jesus love will make you shine
and cause the devil to run behind
Jesus lost his life you see
to give us life and set us free
If not for him we wouldn't be
We need to love him more you see
His love is real and cost no fee
He wants our love whole-heartedly
and not in drips and drabs you see
Who is this Jesus the world needs
to see who gave his life to set us free
The color of him no one will see
He loves us like a rainbow you see
A daddy to all the will always be

Printed in the United States
17341LVS00002B/37-117